Where Is Pennsylvania?

HOME OF

PUNXSY
PHIL

Where Is Pennsylvania?

by Annette Whipple

illustrated by Ted Hammond

Penguin Workshop

For Mom and Dad—
who raised me in Pennsylvania—AW

PENGUIN WORKSHOP
An imprint of Penguin Random House LLC
1745 Broadway, New York, NY 10019
penguinrandomhouse.com

Designed and Produced by Dinardo Design, LLC.

Library of Congress Cataloging-in-Publication Data is available.

First published in the United States of America by Penguin Workshop, 2025

Manufactured in the United States of America
CJKW

ISBN 9798217051434 (paperback)
10 9 8 7 6 5 4 3 2 1

ISBN 9798217051441 (library binding)
10 9 8 7 6 5 4 3 2 1

The authorized representative in the EU for product safety and compliance is
Penguin Random House Ireland, Morrison Chambers, 32 Nassau Street,
Dublin D02 YH68, Ireland, https://eu-contact.penguin.ie.

Contents

Where Is Pennsylvania? 1

Early Pennsylvania 3

Pennsylvania Grows 16

The Making of Modern Pennsylvania 28

Pennsylvania Today 34

Pennsylvania at a Glance 46

Timelines 48

Bibliography. 50

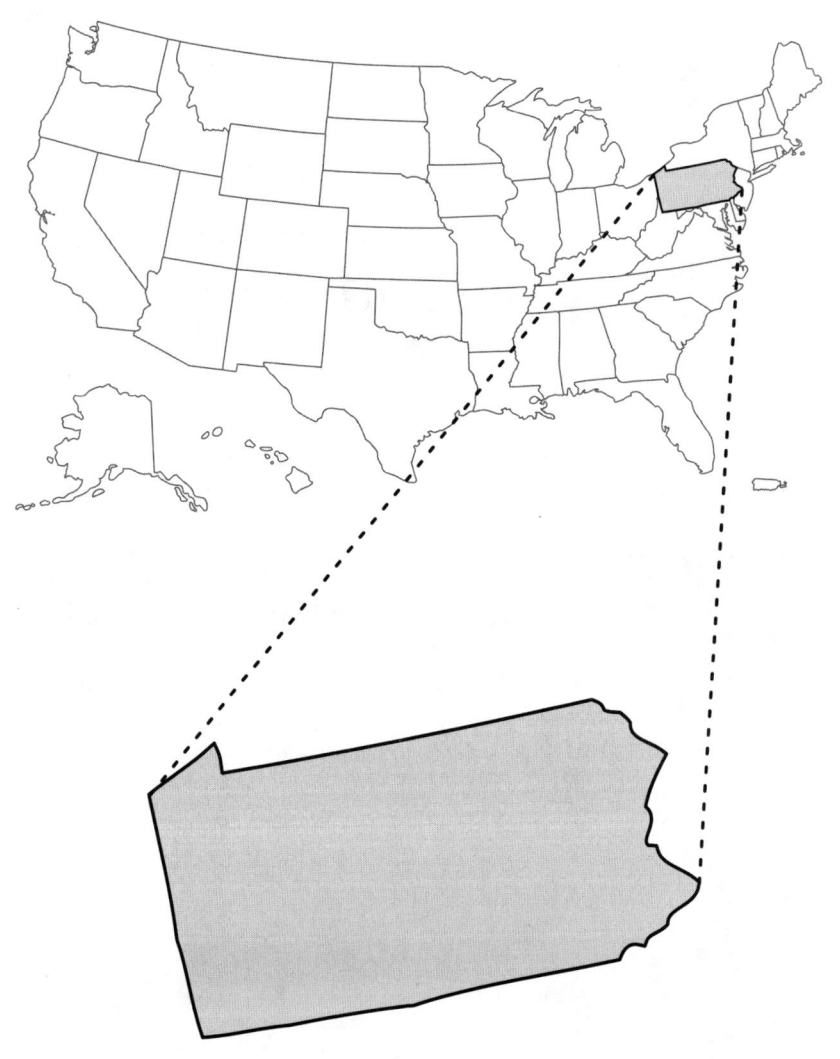

Where Is Pennsylvania?

In 1976, a popular movie called *Rocky* told the story of an Italian American boxer from Philadelphia, Pennsylvania, getting the chance to fight the world heavyweight champion. Rocky is the underdog—very unlikely to win—but he tries anyway. He trains hard to get ready, easily running up the seventy-two steps of the Philadelphia Museum of Art and raising his fists. He's ready to take on his opponent—and the world.

The boxing match takes place in Philadelphia as part of the Bicentennial, or two hundredth anniversary, of the United States of America's independence. The Declaration of Independence was signed in Philadelphia, in a building called Independence Hall, in 1776. In 1976, these celebrations were happening in real life, not just the movie!

Today, there is a statue of Rocky at the bottom of the Philadelphia Museum of Art steps. Nearby, Independence Hall still stands. Two hundred years apart, both represent the spirit of determination that built Pennsylvania and have inspired generations to dream against all odds.

CHAPTER 1
Early Pennsylvania

The year was 1681, and William Penn had an unusual opportunity. King Charles II of England (also known as Britain) owed Penn's family a lot of money. Since the King didn't have much money, he offered Penn land in North America instead. The king's debt was paid with about forty thousand square miles of forested land along the Delaware River. That land would one day form part of the state of Pennsylvania.

At the time of William Penn's arrival, almost all the land was covered with forests. With animals to hunt for food, soil good for growing crops, and many streams and rivers, it had everything people needed to live. The land was filled with hills and mountains, including what are known today as the

Blue Ridge Mountains and Allegheny Mountains. Forests covered flat-topped mountains known today as the Poconos in the eastern part of the state. But it wasn't all mountains: William Penn lived in southeastern Pennsylvania, which was near sea level and rather flat.

The Delaware River ran through the land. Today, the river forms the eastern border of

Pennsylvania along the states of New York and New Jersey. The Susquehanna River flows south through Pennsylvania until it empties into the Chesapeake Bay. Pennsylvania's third major river is the Ohio. The city of Pittsburgh now stands at the meeting of the Ohio with two other rivers. Lake Erie, one of the Great Lakes, forms the border between Pennsylvania and Canada.

Pennsylvania summers are often hot and humid. Fall brings bright colors as the leaves change. Most of the state has cold and even harsh winters. When William Penn arrived, white-tailed deer, ruffed grouse, and fireflies thrived in dense forests as well as fields. Brook trout lived in small creeks, rushing rivers, and lakes. Eastern hellbenders, a kind of amphibian, lived in cold, clear streams. Today, Pennsylvania's state animals share the land with many more people than they did when Penn arrived.

Indigenous people lived in Pennsylvania for thousands of years before William Penn traveled there. The Lenape (say: la-NAH-pay) was the first and largest nation to live in what is known today as eastern Pennsylvania. Lenape people lived in small villages where they hunted, fished, farmed, and foraged. They also made clothing, jewelry, and furniture. In their language of Unami (say: YOO-nah-mee), *Lenape* means "The People."

The Iroquois (say: IR-ah-kwoi) Confederacy lived on the land known today as Pennsylvania and included the Seneca (say: SE-ni-kah), Erie, and Oneida (say: OH-nigh-dah) Nations. They lived in longhouses (wooden homes up to one hundred feet long). As many as sixty people lived in each one. Iroquois people created villages with many longhouses near one another and celebrated forms of art like storytelling and music. The Iroquois people spoke multiple languages.

Other Indigenous groups, such as the Monongahela (say: mah-nahn-gah-HEE-la), Shawnee, and Susquehannock (say: suh-skwah-HAN-nok) Nations, also lived in this region.

William Penn had a plan for this land he'd been given by the king. He wanted to form a new colony and call it *Sylvania* (which means "forest" in Latin). The king wished to honor Penn's father, so they agreed to call the colony Pennsylvania.

William Penn was a Quaker. Quakerism is a

Christian religious movement that was founded in England in the 1650s. Penn's Quaker beliefs meant he believed in the equality of all people, and he opposed war. The British government did not agree with the Quakers. Penn was jailed four times for his beliefs, even though he knew the king. Penn wanted Pennsylvania to welcome all people, including Quakers and those of other faiths.

By this time, the land already had European settlements. Henry Hudson was one of the first Europeans to visit Pennsylvania when he sailed up the Delaware River in 1609. A few years later, more people arrived. At first, Lenape representatives allowed for a temporary Dutch settlement and welcomed trade with settlers. People from Sweden, the Netherlands, and Britain came to live on the land. The colonists brought diseases that killed many Indigenous people, and they often didn't honor the agreements they had made with Indigenous nations.

Penn wanted Pennsylvania to be a safe place for the Lenape and other Indigenous peoples. He made new laws. Penn and Chief Tamanend of the Lenape signed many treaties, or agreements, together. One formalized the purchase of land from the Lenape people and declared peace, which both Chief Tamanend and William Penn wanted. Penn paid for the land with goods that the chief shared with the Lenape.

Penn's plan brought even more immigrants to Pennsylvania. Colonists came from Britain, Scotland, Holland, Germany, and Ireland. Penn founded a city called Philadelphia. As children were born across the colony, the European population grew.

When William Penn died in 1718, his son Thomas was left in charge of the colony. He didn't practice the same Quaker religion as his father. He tricked the Lenape into giving land to

Pennsylvania. Britain wanted more land for the colonies, too. They fought France over it from 1754 to 1763 in a conflict called the French and Indian War. When Britain won the war, they claimed even more land for Pennsylvania.

European and colonial leaders wanted more space and made agreements without respect for Lenape leaders, expelling them from their land. As the settler population increased, food became more scarce. Indigenous groups had to find new hunting grounds and resources to survive.

Like the other colonies in North America, Pennsylvania was ruled by Britain. Over time, Britain and its king asked colonists to pay higher taxes while refusing to give them any say in the British government or its laws. In 1774, representatives from twelve colonies met in Philadelphia for the First Continental Congress. The group wrote a letter to King George III about their concerns. The British king ignored the letter. So they wrote another. The king and government still didn't listen. Most colonists agreed they would have to separate from Britain. That meant war.

The American Revolution began in 1775. The next year, a group including Thomas Jefferson, John Adams, and Benjamin Franklin once again met in Philadelphia to write a letter from the thirteen colonies to the king. This letter was called the Declaration of Independence and explained why the colonies wanted to be free from Britain. It listed the ways the British government and their king had been unfair to colonists and introduced the name of their new country: United States of America.

The thirteen colonies became a nation on July 4, 1776. *Clang! Clang! Clang!* A three-foot-tall bell rang out in Philadelphia to announce freedom from Britain and celebrate the first public reading of the Declaration of Independence. Known

today as the Liberty Bell, it is a favorite stop for visitors from around the world.

The British didn't want to give up their land or the money they took through taxation. The countries continued to battle for years. On September 11, 1777, the Revolutionary War came to Pennsylvania. The Battle of Brandywine was the largest one-day battle of the war. As many as thirty thousand soldiers participated. The outnumbered colonist soldiers, called the Continental army, lost. But the Battle of Brandywine proved their toughness and convinced France to support them. France's decision changed the outcome of the war.

The commander in chief of the Continental army, George Washington, withdrew from Philadelphia. The army set up camp in Valley Forge, about twenty miles from the city. The soldiers built log huts. Each cabin housed about twenty men but was only fourteen by sixteen feet in size! They built miles of trenches, paths,

and roads. It was a brutally cold winter, and the army had very few warm clothes or shoes. Straw from local fields was used for bedding since there weren't enough blankets. The army was running out of food.

Finally, help arrived. A German baker wisely used a small amount of flour to make as much bread as possible. With training and support from France, the Continental army became a fighting

force. They learned new skills and fought as a unified force.

The war lasted until 1783 when the United States of America finally won their freedom. Pennsylvania officially became a state when its representatives signed the US Constitution in 1787.

CHAPTER 2
Pennsylvania Grows

The United States established itself as a new country, and the population of Pennsylvania grew. While many families still farmed in rural areas, some moved to busy cities where there were opportunities to work in government, shipping, and other industries. Throughout the 1800s, manufacturing (businesses that change raw materials into goods) increased.

Pennsylvania was centrally located and important in politics and industry. It earned a nickname: the Keystone State. A keystone is the wedge-shaped piece at the top of a stone arch that holds the structure together. Thanks to its place at the heart of the nation, the hard work of its citizens, and the many natural resources of its land, Pennsylvania played a central role in the growth of the United States.

European immigrants continued to arrive and contribute to the economy. Many worked in steel mills or coal mines. Others made fabrics, textiles, or ships. Railroads shipped the many products made and mined in Pennsylvania across the country. Lake Erie's port and the state's rivers were also important in transporting Pennsylvania goods.

Just as Europeans came to Pennsylvania for work, so did people from other parts of America, including Black people seeking freedom from enslavement in the southern states. By the mid-1800s the southern boundary of Pennsylvania was the dividing line between the free states in the north and the slave states in the south. The border was called the Mason-Dixon Line. Crossing it meant the first step to escape for many enslaved Black freedom seekers.

Throughout the country, the Underground Railroad secretly assisted enslaved people fleeing from the American south to Canada. Those working on the Underground Railroad provided safe places with food, shelter, information, and a connection to the next station. Participating in the Underground Railroad was illegal and life-threatening, yet every county in Pennsylvania had at least one location.

Just twelve miles from the Mason-Dixon line in West Grove, Pennsylvania, Dr. Ann Preston's home was a major station on the Underground Railroad. Dr. Preston, a white Quaker woman, provided medical care to freedom seekers in her home, as well as food and shelter. It was common for her to take freedom seekers by carriage to the next station. They had to avoid—or outwit—the slave patrol (people who made a living tracking down and chasing freedom seekers to return them to their enslaver for a fee). On one trip, Preston's freedom-seeking companion was dressed in Quaker clothing (like Preston's own). The patrol

thought they were just out for a ride. The disguise worked!

A woman named Harriet Tubman had been enslaved in Maryland since her birth. After she escaped to Philadelphia, she used her knowledge of the south to help others. Harriet was the most famous Underground Railroad conductor and worked with many connections in Pennsylvania. She led as many as three hundred people to freedom, including her own parents.

By 1860, nearly fifty-seven thousand Black people lived in Pennsylvania. All were free. They often looked to the city of Philadelphia for opportunities. Many were only offered low-paying jobs, including at the city's docks. Others became schoolteachers, church ministers, or restaurant waiters. James Forten was a Black businessman with a successful sailmaking business.

Eventually southern states decided to secede,

or leave, the United States. Rather than outlaw slavery, they formed their own country called the Confederate States of America (also known as the Confederacy). The Civil War began in 1861, with Pennsylvania on the border of the two nations.

In July 1863, a three-day fight in Gettysburg, Pennsylvania, changed the outcome of the war. Before the Battle of Gettysburg, the Confederate army had won many fights. People worried that the Union, or the North, would lose the war. At Gettysburg, the Union prevailed and the Confederacy lost more than one-third of their whole army.

Four months after the Battle of Gettysburg, about fifteen thousand people gathered there to dedicate the Soldiers' National Cemetery in memory of those who had died in the fighting. President Abraham Lincoln shared a powerful speech called the Gettysburg Address which

focused on national unity while honoring the
deaths and sacrifices of the soldiers who fought at
Gettysburg.

The fighting continued until the Union won
the Civil War in 1865. The United States became
one country again. Slavery was outlawed in every
state. In many places and especially in the south,
violence and unfair laws still made life very

difficult for Black people. Many moved north, and some went to Pennsylvania.

The state also welcomed more immigrants: Italians, Poles, Russians, and Hungarians came to live on farms and in small towns and to work in cities. Some did not work in factories or buildings—they worked underground.

By the late 1800s, one of Pennsylvania's biggest

industries was coal mining. Mine workers had to dig out coal from tunnels deep underground. The mines were dark, dirty, and damp. In northeastern Pennsylvania, the city of Scranton became a hub for coal mining and railroad routes. Between 1860 and 1900, its population increased rapidly as immigrants, many of them Irish, arrived. Men worked in coal mines, digging, drilling by hand, and blasting walls. They loaded up coal cars (like carts), so ponies and mules could haul them out of the mine. Coal mining was dangerous. Many miners were injured or killed. Others developed health problems from breathing coal dust.

Coal was shipped by railroad to power many homes and businesses across America. It was also important to the steel industry. Pittsburgh, a city in southwestern Pennsylvania, became known as "Steel City." The city's location was ideal since there was so much coal and iron ore (a mineral also used to make steel) being mined nearby. The

three rivers of Pittsburgh provided quick and easy transportation of the steel the city produced. Pittsburgh's steel mills began using the successful Bessemer process, a new method that made steel stronger, faster, and cheaper.

With northeastern Pennsylvania's coal mines making the area a center of industry, the Delaware, Lackawanna and Western Railroad Company built a bridge to make its rails more efficient. In

1915, the Tunkhannock Creek Viaduct, a concrete bridge designed for trains, was completed. It was built by about five hundred men (with very few tools). They used 185,000 barrels of concrete and over 1,000 tons of steel to create the 2,375-foot-long railroad bridge. The bridge still carries trains today! Its arches are long—ten are nearly 200 feet long—and it towers 240 feet above the water.

CHAPTER 3
The Making of Modern Pennsylvania

Pennsylvania's growth in industry led to factories focusing on food products. This has resulted in a history of food built around unlikely and groundbreaking snacks.

In 1861, in the town of Lititz, Pennsylvania, Julius Sturgis developed crispy pretzels in America's first pretzel bakery. Snackers still enjoy pretzels made in the Julius Sturgis Pretzel Bakery and other factories all over the state. Today, 80 percent of the nation's pretzels are made in Pennsylvania!

After tasting milk chocolate in Europe, Milton Hershey wanted Americans to have a chance to enjoy the delicious treat. He experimented and worked for years to perfect his recipe for milk chocolate. In 1894, Hershey established the Hershey Chocolate Company and eventually became one of the leading chocolate makers in the world. The Hershey's chocolate bar was the first mass-produced chocolate bar in the United States, which meant it was more accessible, and more people could afford to buy it. This changed the candy industry.

After building his chocolate-making factory in 1905, Milton Hershey used his success to create a model town for his employees. In addition to the factory, the town included homes, a transportation system, and even a school system. In 1909, he established the Hershey Industrial School (now called the Milton Hershey School), a private school for orphan boys.

Milton Hershey

Today, visitors can enjoy nearby Hersheypark, stroll Hershey Gardens, and take the chocolate tour. Milton Hershey is still known around the world for his chocolate.

Pennsylvania is also known for its famous cheesesteaks, which originated in Philadelphia. Made of beef and melted cheese on a long, soft roll, no one is sure of who exactly invented the

cheesesteak, but many believe that it was Pat and Harry Olivieri. The brothers popularized the cheesesteak sandwich at their hot dog stand in the early 1930s. Whoever invented them, the cheesesteak is still one of the most popular foods in Philadelphia!

If the Olivieri family did invent the famous sandwich, they did it in a time when people needed cheering up: The Great Depression had begun in 1929. The Great Depression was a period during which the US and other countries suffered a severe financial crisis. Many banks and businesses failed and there were high rates of unemployment.

By 1930, factories and mills employed nearly a million people in Pennsylvania. During the Great Depression, more than five thousand factories and mills closed. Many people in Pennsylvania lost their jobs. It was especially difficult for some of Pennsylvania's towns and counties where one industry—like coal or steel—was the major employer. When coal mines and steel mills shut down, people were left with no money to buy food or clothing. Paying for rent or medicine became more difficult, and as a result, people like store owners, doctors, and teachers were also affected.

While many cities in the state, including the largest, Philadelphia, faced an unemployment crisis during the Great Depression, people in rural areas fared a bit better. Farmers were used to growing their own food and living off of the land. Still, joblessness and poverty reached rural areas, too.

In order to assist people, the US government set up charities and work programs. In the early 1940s, when World War II began, factories began to produce much-needed goods like tanks, parachutes, and battleships. Many of these ships were made of Pennsylvania steel. People had jobs again. With over a million Pennsylvania men serving in the military, women started doing factory work to keep up with the war demand.

As the state of Pennsylvania grew, colleges were needed to educate people. Universities like Lehigh, Villanova, and Pennsylvania State University were all founded in the mid-1800s. The University of Pittsburgh was founded in 1787 and is one of the oldest institutions of higher learning in the country. The Ashmun Institute (now called Lincoln University) was the first degree-granting Historically Black College and University (HBCU) in the country.

Education was important to business owners in Pennsylvania. They wanted educated workers to help them grow and adapt to changing times and innovation. Businesses in Pennsylvania used and developed new technologies to continue producing goods for the world to use. Today, Pennsylvania provides food and products to the country and the world.

CHAPTER 4
Pennsylvania Today

Coal and steel are still a part of Pennsylvania's economy. As technology has changed, oil, natural gas, and electricity have also become important to the energy industry. Today, Pennsylvania is the second-largest energy producer in the US. Batteries, aircraft, and metal goods are also produced in the state. Pennsylvania contributes to the aerospace, transportation, and defense industries.

The H. J. Heinz Company (now the Kraft Heinz Company) was founded in Pennsylvania in 1869 and is still headquartered in Pittsburgh. While the company now sells more than five thousand products, it is probably best known for its famous Heinz ketchup. Pennsylvania manufactures other famous products, too, including Harley-Davidson motorcycles and Crayola crayons.

In addition to manufacturing, agriculture (farming) continues to be a major industry in Pennsylvania. Pennsylvania has about five thousand dairy farms and is ranked eighth in milk production nationwide. Its farms produce about ten billion pounds of milk each year! It's no wonder that milk is the state beverage. Farmers in Pennsylvania also raise chickens, beef cattle, and hogs. Corn and soybeans are top agricultural products, as are apples and peaches. Pennsylvania is also one of the biggest producers of mushrooms in the country. Pennsylvania produces more mushrooms than any other state—450 million pounds each year!

Today, about thirteen million people live across Pennsylvania in its thriving cities and small towns. Residents frequently refer to their home state by its initials: PA (say: PEE-ay). Pennsylvania

has a diverse population. About thirty thousand people from various Indigenous nations live in Pennsylvania. Throughout the state, gatherings called powwows involve singing, dancing, food, and crafts. These events are used to remember and celebrate Indigenous traditions, languages, and culture. Pennsylvania is one of the few states whose government does not officially recognize its Indigenous groups (past or present). The Lenape

people are working to change that through petitions, raising awareness, and outreach to local legislators.

The people of Pennsylvania and its visitors enjoy cultural experiences with its theaters, museums, and concerts. Many famous people are from Pennsylvania, including the actors James Stewart, Sharon Stone, and Will Smith, and singers Taylor Swift and Billie Holiday. Pennsylvania county fairs show off farm animals, crafts, and baked goods while providing entertainment with music, tractor pulls, and rodeos. Festivals celebrate a variety of interests ranging from art and winter holidays to mushrooms and UFOs! Other events showcase cars (both new and old), flowers, and farm equipment.

Well-known artists such as Keith Haring, Andy Warhol, and Mary Cassatt were born in Pennsylvania, and the Philadelphia Museum of Art displays masterpieces from around the world. Visitors can climb the same steps that fictional boxer Rocky ran up in the movie *Rocky*, and pose at the top with his statue. Other museums in the state explore local industries, like coal, and Amish (say: AH-mish) culture.

The Amish are a religious group who originally came to Pennsylvania because it welcomed different religions. Their first settlement in Lancaster began in the early 1700s, and many

Amish people still live there today. Their beliefs require them to live simply, without electricity or other modern conveniences like computers or cars. When traveling locally, Amish people use a horse and buggy (similar to a carriage).

Pennsylvania has 124 state parks with more than three hundred thousand acres. The state's beautiful outdoor areas are appreciated by people who hike trails, kayak rivers, and explore the countryside. One local animal in Pennsylvania has become famous for his predictions about the weather. On February 2 each year, thousands of curious people arrive in the western town of Punxsutawney (say: punk-suh-TAW-nee) to celebrate Groundhog Day. According to legend, if the famous groundhog Punxsutawney Phil sees his shadow, winter will last six more weeks. If he doesn't, spring will arrive early.

Sports are big in Pennsylvania. Each summer, Pennsylvania hosts the Little League World

Series—a baseball tournament for children ages ten to twelve who come from teams all over the country and all over the world.

Jim Thorpe (1887–1953)

Jim Thorpe was born in Oklahoma. He was a member of the Sac and Fox Nation. His Sac name was Wa-tho-Huck, which means "bright path." Jim was sent to a boarding  school by a government agency, like many Indigenous children at the time. These schools were designed to "teach" Indigenous children to act, speak, and dress like white Americans, and they often abused and mistreated the students in their care. Unsurprisingly, Jim didn't like school. While at boarding school, Jim's twin brother died of pneumonia. Jim tried to run away many times.

Eventually, Jim went to Carlisle Indian Industrial School in Pennsylvania. Carlisle was still a boarding school for Indigenous children, but it had athletic programs. Jim joined the track-and-field and football teams. He spent years at Carlisle and cared deeply for his coach and teammates. Eventually, he was named to the All-American first football team and trained to compete in the Olympics.

At the 1912 Olympic games in Sweden, Jim won gold in the pentathlon and decathlon. People in America and around the globe celebrated Jim as one of the best athletes in the world. Although he faced racism and other obstacles, Jim went on to play both baseball and football professionally and was named to the Pro Football Hall of Fame. After his death, he was named the number one athlete of the twentieth century by the US Congress.

Today, Jim Thorpe is remembered in Pennsylvania and around the world as one of the greatest athletes ever. There is even a town named after him—Jim Thorpe, Pennsylvania.

Sports fans in Pennsylvania also root for professional teams. Passionate Pittsburgh fans root for the Steelers (football), Penguins (ice hockey), and Pirates (baseball). Philadelphia's enthusiastic crowds cheer on the Eagles (football), Union (soccer), Flyers (ice hockey), Phillies (baseball), and 76ers (basketball). Athletes Kobe Bryant, Joe Montana, and Jim Thorpe have all lived in the Keystone State. Two-time Olympic archer Casey Kaufhold is from Lancaster.

About thirteen million people call the Keystone State their home. Millions more visit as tourists. William Penn wouldn't recognize the former colony he founded—but it's still Pennsylvania, where all are welcomed and people with big dreams take on the world.

Pennsylvania at a Glance

Statehood: 1787

Nickname: The Keystone State

Abbreviation: PA

State Motto: Virtue, Liberty, and Independence

State Tree: Eastern hemlock

State Animal: White-tailed deer

Capital: Harrisburg

Size: 46,055 square miles

Population: Over 13 million

Famous People from Pennsylvania:

Louisa May Alcott (author), Marian Anderson (contralto singer), Fred Rogers (Mister Rogers), Quinta Brunson (actress and writer), Martha Graham (choreographer)

State flag

State bird
Ruffed grouse

State flower
Mountain laurel

FUN FACT:

A seven-mile hiking trail in Ricketts Glen State Park contains twenty-one waterfalls. The tallest waterfall is the ninety-four-foot-tall Ganoga Falls.

Timeline of Pennsylvania

1609	Henry Hudson visits the land of Pennsylvania
1681	William Penn founds the colony of Pennsylvania
1718	William Penn dies
1774	First Continental Congress meetings take place in Philadelphia
1775	The Revolutionary War begins between Britain and the thirteen colonies
	Second Continental Congress meetings take place in Philadelphia
1776	Declaration of Independence is written in Philadelphia
1787	Pennsylvania becomes a state
1812	Harrisburg becomes the state capital
1863	The Battle of Gettysburg is fought
1865	The American Civil War ends
1939	World War II begins
1976	The movie *Rocky* is the highest grossing film in the world
1989	Taylor Swift is born near Reading, Pennsylvania
2024	Lake Mary, Florida, wins the Little League World Series near Williamsport, Pennsylvania

Timeline of the World

1607	Jamestown in the colony of Virginia is founded
1718	The city of New Orleans is founded
1775	Alexander Cumming invents the flushable toilet
1821	Panama, Guatemala, and Santo Domingo gain independence from Spain
1876	Alexander Graham Bell invents the telephone
1893	The Chicago World's Fair includes the first presentations of the Ferris wheel and electricity
1903	Wilbur and Orville Wright invent and fly the first airplane
1914	The Panama Canal is completed, connecting the Atlantic and Pacific Oceans
1918	World War I ends
1939	World War II begins
1969	Neil Armstrong becomes the first person to walk on the moon
1991	The World Wide Web is invented
1994	Nelson Mandela becomes president of South Africa
2024	About 15,000 Olympic and Paralympic athletes compete in the Summer Olympics and Paralympics hosted in Paris, France

Bibliography

*Books for young readers

*Buckley, James, Jr. *Who Was Milton Hershey?* New York: Penguin Workshop, 2013.

"Continental Congress." *Britannica Kids*. kids.britannica.com/kids/article/Continental- Congress/352998.

*Harris, Michael C. *What Was the Declaration of Independence?* New York: Penguin Workshop, 2016.

*Kellaher, Karen. *Pennsylvania*. My United States. New York: Children's Press, 2019.

"Maps of Pennsylvania." *World Atlas*. www.worldatlas.com/maps/united-states/pennsylvania.

Miller, Randall M., and William Pencak, eds. *Pennsylvania: A History of the Commonwealth*. University Park, Pennsylvania: The Pennsylvania State University Press; Harrisburg, Pennsylvania: The Pennsylvania Historical and Museum Commission, 2002.

"Pennsylvania." *Britannica*. www.britannica.com/place/Pennsylvania-state.

"Pennsylvania Facts & History." *Visit Pennsylvania*. www.visitpa.com/facts-and-history.

*Somervill, Barbara A. *Pennsylvania*. America the Beautiful. Third Series New York: Scholastic, Inc., 2015.

Website

Lenape Nation: lenape-nation.org